KES'ALUL

I place you

KES'ALUL

into the fire

KE'SA LUL

POEMS

REBECCA THOMAS

NIMBUS
PUBLISHING
NIMBUS.CA

T0026886

Nimbus Publishing Limited
3660 Strawberry Hill Street, Halifax, NS, B3K 5A9
(902) 455-4286 nimbus.ca

Printed and bound in Canada

NB1415

Editor: Whitney Moran
Design: Jenn Embree

"Creature Canada" was originally delivered as a Walrus Talk in Halifax, NS, May 12, 2017. "Canoe" was written for the National Trustee Gathering on Aboriginal Education, July 2018. "DMJ" was written for and originally delivered at Dalhousie University Schulich School of Law's "Honouring the Life and Continuing the Work of Donald Marshall Jr.," December 15, 2017. "It's Your Turn" was written, as "Saltwire," for the Saltwire Network and the RISE series, spring 2019.

Library and Archives Canada Cataloguing in Publication

Title: I place you into the fire / Rebecca Thomas.
Names: Thomas, Rebecca (Poet), author.
Description: Poems.
Identifiers: Canadiana (print) 2020026527X | Canadiana (ebook) 20200265288 | ISBN 9781771088855 (softcover) | ISBN 9781771088862 (EPUB)
Classification: LCC PS8639.H5875 I2 2020 | DDC C811/.6—dc23

Nimbus Publishing acknowledges the financial support for its publishing activities from the Government of Canada, the Canada Council for the Arts, and from the Province of Nova Scotia. We are pleased to work in partnership with the Province of Nova Scotia to develop and promote our creative industries for the benefit of all Nova Scotians.

kesalul
("I love you")

kesa'lul
("I hurt you")

ke'sa'lul
("I place you into the fire")

Contents

KeSALuL

("I love you")

Ribbons

I used to have magic.
It made airplanes fly and the sky blue.
My magic turned raindrops into rainbows.
It made me special.
It was my suit of armour against the world.
I-spy champion, invisible companions,
and no-take-backsies extraordinaire:
think you could beat me? I'd answer you with a double-dog dare
and the most intimidating stare a six-year-old could muster.

My magic prepared me
for a career as a veterinarian, astronaut, dinosaur discoverer.
An uncoverer of secret nooks and crannies with pockets full
of beach sand, lint, and sour candies.

My magic turned the bruises that covered my arms and legs
into constellations and galaxies completely removed
from context.
It made me resilient and unaware of subtext.

My magic separated feminism from concept.
I wasn't the lesser sex; I could inspect my body and see no flaws
because it looked just like my mom's.
And after all, she was my hero.

She was the man of the house.
Pardon the metaphor, but in this day and age it still tends to carry
a lot more clout.
Because in spite of all her achievements she still felt compelled
to take the name of her spouse.

Doused in the harsh reality of a doctor called nurse,
she set her magic aside and put us first.

I remember the first time my magic flickered.
The breath of my disappointed sigh reached out to caress its flame.
At eight years old, with tears in my eyes, and in hers, pain,
I explained that the tooth fairy, a woman I believed in,
never came.
You see, I had slipped the tooth under my pillow
without ever telling my mom.
I wasn't too old to believe, no kid on the playground broke the story,
no tragic allegory.
Just a working mom so tired from trying to give us a healthy lifestyle
that she completely missed the gap in the smile
of her youngest child.

With that, my magic started to fade.
I learned how to shave. I was told how a woman should behave.
But the hair under my arms says I've never been good
at playing that game.

So I'm going to let you in on a little secret:
holding onto my magic has always been a bit of a weakness.
I don't believe in the traditional roles set out for me
as told by books about Jesus, a right-wing thesis,
or makeup commercials that insist we are all made up
of our own special uniqueness—
as long as we buy their specially formulated treatment.
My magic is frequent.

It isn't fair.
Even though it is still there, my magic was not strong enough
to protect them.

I wear a purple ribbon over the source of my magic
to remember them.
I send a message that we and her and she and all the iterations
of the feminine are worth a thousand times more
than the collective thoughts of angry men.

My magic, fortified by theirs, made me believe I could be anything.
So, without further ado world,
here I am.

One of Those Families

I come from one of those families
where the mothers burn out
where the fathers check out
where child support was too hard
but money kept flowing for the tab at the bar.
I come from one of those families
where we drove a used car and she missed my recitals
where my uncle escaped with a gun to his vitals.

I come from one of those families
where my mom was a doctor and I was captain of the track team,
but always was told I'd have to fight for my dream.
I come from one of those families
where everything I loved had conditions.
where praise was a handout that was limited edition.
I come from one of those families
that history split up
and left us wondering if we'd ever be enough.

I come from one of those families
where we didn't have choices,
but were consistently told the world was our oyster.
I come from one of those families
where my friends couldn't understand
why my mom was so white, but I was so tan.

I come from one of those families
where promises were broken
where hurt was endured but never spoken.

I come from one of those families
where we solved our problems with our fists,
but ended every night with a hug and a kiss.

I come from one of those families
where the kids stepped up when something was off
where our skin got thick and our hearts grew soft.
I come from one of those families
where the meals were served with regret
once a week on my grandfather's china set.

I come from one of those families
where we all went to university,
we all got degrees.
We had to be miserable to be seen,
attention garnered only when we bleed.

I come from one of those families
where we had to be better.
I come from one of those families that understood "never."
I come from one of those families
that looked good from far away,
where sons and daughters silently cried for their father to stay.
We didn't get that he kept history at bay.
I come from one of those families
where we don't talk much
where we never really learned affection and touch.

I come from one of those families
that slowly broke open
where we dug out holes to plant our hopes in.

I come from one of those families
where we bleed forgiveness.

With just enough privilege
to play devil's advocate to my heritage.

I come from one of those families
where we inherited burdens that made our backs strong
where we hold on to our baggage so we don't pass it along.
I come from one of those families
where we're looked on with pity
where you can hang out and then leave feeling guilty.
I come from one of those families
where we are extended and vast
where we try so hard not to repeat the past.
I come from one of those families
where people look at us and "tisk"
because they don't get how much we have risked.
I come from one of those families that are multicoloured.
I come from one of those families that always gave shelter.
I come from one of those families that are like no other.
I come from one of those families raised by the mothers.
I come from one of those families with too many kids.
I come from one of those families that just wants to live.
I come from one of those families.

Fuck Buns

Opening the fridge door,
I spy what I'm looking for.
The 99-cent pack of hot dogs and Heinz ketchup that was always
a staple in a house that was constantly running out of milk.
The mustard could be No Name, French's, or some other off brand.
It didn't matter, it was all about the ketchup.
When times were dire, you still had to know how to treat yourself.
But the mustard had to be neon yellow with enough vinegar
to polish silver.

There are those who boil hot dogs or fry them in a pan,
but in this under-supervised, overstretched house
it was 1:23 in the microwave on thrift-store dishes—
assuming there were clean dishes;
otherwise, those bad boys went on nothing.
The results were the same.
We didn't fuck with buns.
A couple of slices of Wonder Bread—
except it wasn't Wonder Bread;
it was the grocery-store version that would disappear in a day—
folded in half around Cheez Whiz, peanut butter, or in this case,
hot dogs.
Like I said, we didn't fuck with buns.

We had to have more than a single talent.
We had to be multifaceted in our skill set
if we were to ever make it out of that house.
We had to rise and grind,
be toast for breakfast.
A little burnt, but you just had to scrape that off.

There were no do-overs.
Nothing went to waste.
We had to carry it all and be thick-skinned enough
for a sandwich at lunch,
holding in the too much that was put on us.
And we had to be grilled cheese for dinner,
dipped in Campbell's tomato soup—
except it wasn't Campbell's;
it was No Name, but it got the job done
without all the compliments.
We carried around our food on paper towels
since the dishes weren't clean—except it wasn't paper towel;
it was a couple pieces of toilet paper stashed on top of the fridge
next to the Scotch tape in case we needed tissues or a Band-Aid.
We sat in front of the TV eating our supper, watching sitcoms like
Family Matters, *Full House*, and *Boy Meets World*, with their
name-brand things, clean dishes, and parents.
We wondered what it was like to live in a fairy tale.

I still prefer microwaved hot dogs on bread.
I don't buy buns, because I know better.

A Toast to The Mixes

This is a toast!
So raise a glass:
To the halves,
to the mixes.
The "My dad is this,"
the "My mom is that."
To the "I didn't grow up there,"
to the "She's where I get my hair,"
and "I have his eyes and her size."
To the 50/50s!
To this fucked-up identity purgatory.
I got you.

To the "That's not how I expected you to sound,"
which translates to "I'm only comfortable with you because
you're not all the way brown."
To the just a little too dark,
to the just the right amount of exotic
to play the ambiguously ethnic, sexualized part.
To the "You're really attractive for a Native,"
as though this is a compliment that will get me naked.
To the many census boxes to tick,
knowing they only care about one side if it lays claim
to the Arctic.
To the race politics that break your heart.
To the community where you so desperately want to be a part.
I got you.

To the overcompensation
and uncertain call-outs of cultural appropriation.

To the self-altering just to get recognized instead of questioned.
To wishing you had a more Native inflection.
A darker complexion.
Straighter hair.
Or were maybe a little less socially aware.
To being a disarming shade of brown.
To having your credibility cut down.
To the "You're not like the rest of them"—
and yet still you're drawn as a stereotype
by those who hold the pen.

Pour a little out for the misplaced blame.
Cheers to being shamed for not knowing
something you were never taught.
That culture is something precious, that it can't be bought.
And here's to being left tear-streaked and seething.
As though guarding endangered words makes a person special,
instead of greedy.
To having one sharp statement cut you down to a child playing
cultural dress-up.
To being at fault for your insufficient genetic makeup.
To being an open wound, instead of an open book.
To being told, "You don't quite have that look."
To not having to search very far to be able to see where I will scar.
And feeling like a token for your company to reach
the diversity bar.
To knowing my white flesh is fragile,
but that my brown skin is resilient and agile.
This is for you.

This is for remarks about your competence
masquerading as conversation—or worse,
a compliment.

To being reduced to fractions and percentages
graphed and other mathematical tools of measurement.
To being on the other end of legitimate and authentic.
This is for the self-doubt etched on your soul.
But in spite of all that shit,
here's to knowing that it takes many ingredients
to make a whole.

WHERE ARE YOU FROM?

I come from a colonized education
and a settler expectation.
I come from protecting my fragile ego,
born afraid of my own people.
I have a lack of jingles.
It's taken years of therapy for my blood to commingle.
I've had to shift my perspective
because building textbook roots was my best elective.
My mocs were designed for city streets,
while I garnished my presence with store-bought beads.
I have thousands of hours spent in universities
instead of learning from the ground under my Elders' feet.
My shawl fringe is bureaucratic red tape.
A series of issued numbers legitimized my state.

But at least I know where I come from.

An Indian Called Sir

I never met the demons that lived inside you.
I didn't even know they were there.
It wasn't that you didn't care about us or cared about it more.
You wore your scars on the inside.
When you were struggling, you would hide.

I would get letters from you in lieu of yourself.
Never cries for help but handwritten determination
that in spite of what you were facing, I would never doubt your love.

I remember telling all my friends that you would come
to my birthday.
That you would come home and stay, that we would play.
We made a deal, you made a promise.
I told my friends that you were real!

I was eight, maybe ten, when you made it.
You didn't just say it, you were there.
I was trying on the lipstick my friend gave me as a gift,
having no idea how to properly paint my lips,
as my older sis dismissed my attempts to be a grown-up,
I turned around, and you had shown up.

To say I was used to the disappointment wouldn't be fair.
I simply didn't expect you to ever be there.
It wasn't as though you weren't missed or loved.
At single digits, I hadn't learned how to judge.
I was so used to justifying your lack of existence
that it caught me off guard
when at your arrival, I started to cry so hard.

Because I missed you.
I missed the idea of you.
I never knew what it was like to have a dad.
I'm sorry for all the times I got mad,
not realizing that deep down,
you were so very sad.

You protected me from your demons.
I don't know about my older siblings, but you made sure
I would never see them.
I was oblivious that you drank to even the sum;
demons couldn't hurt the already numb.
You were trying to give your heart a chance to heal.
You were steeling the strength of your inner child,
the child that you can no longer communicate with
because your language, residential school had wholly stripped.

You are not unique to this struggle,
many parents with your history fumble,
but you still kept me safe inside my bubble.
My ignorance saved my innocence.
Never violence, only forgiveness
when I locked your keys in your car
in a snowstorm
with it running.

I didn't know that alcoholics could be soft and complex.
That drunks were loving, nevertheless.
Lushes loved their kids in spite of their pain,
and boozers could give advice that would help you sustain.
It is for these reasons that I never called you any of those names.

You never abstained from encouragement and applause.
You paused my contempt.

I attempted to hold it against you, that it was my purview;
rent was overdue, the chickens were coming home to roost,
but you knew our relationship could and would not be reduced
to a daughter with daddy issues.

When I was sixteen you gave up the drink,
opting to fight your demons alone.
You began to shed the residue of residential school,
of war, of children lost to a disease you couldn't fight
with your hands.

With each demon you lost, you replaced it with burdens
like guilt
and regret.
You believe you were pre-set to failure,
but time and time again you proved them wrong.
Each child, a song.
We are our own unique successes,
not because of your absence but because of your persistence.
Your insistence on continuing your existence.
You make good kids.
I don't forgive you because there is nothing to forgive.

We have a great father who put his best foot forward
whenever he could.
Yes, there were hiccups and fuck-ups. Missed opportunities and
women with too much makeup.

And even though you might find it absurd,
you have earned your title.
Wear it proudly:
An Indian called Sir.

CHILD

Child, he says.
Child, he calls me.
Child instead of t'us, because residential school
knocked his language loose.
So I am his child as he tries to make a connection.
By passing on dark eyes instead of inflection.
He lost his direction.
His world was gripped by a colonial infection.

Now here I stand,
my feet bruised and bleeding.
The path is well worn from my ancestors,
but it is in need of weeding.

I Wrote You This Poem

You welcomed me into your home,
and told me about the times you felt so alone.
Because of this kindness and trust,
I wrote you this poem.

So many cousins are new to me.
All of these faces are family.
Yet I can't get past my anxiety.
Their laughter, so crisp and clear,
can't assuage my given fear
that I will be less than.
And my achievements won't cover the span
of being away from your and my home,
the one I've never known.
So I wrote you this poem.

The inescapable history that took your sister
shows in the pain I see in how you miss her.
You fed and cared for me,
affection I can clearly see.
And I'm so sorry,
because you were so brave when you told me your story
while I hid mine.
I never told you about the times
when bruises bloomed
and life felt doomed.

When I didn't have a voice from too much crying
from all the lying
about where these marks came from.
And my ability to run,
passed down through my father.

I always criticized him
because I was too much his daughter.
And why I don't like to be touched.
That sometimes care can be too much.
I crave silence
because it used to be a reprieve from the violence,
from skin that took on the colour of violets.
I sometimes forget that I'm now my own pilot.
I carry the baggage that made my back strong.
And to you, I dragged it along.
And still.

You welcomed me into your home,
so I wouldn't be so alone.
So I wrote you this poem.
Next time, I'll take off this mask.
I'll let you take me to task for leaving your home.
Because I needed to be alone.
And when I finally was,
I wrote you this poem.

GRAMPY

The only time I was okay with a man telling me to go
make him a sandwich was the day my grandfather
received his cancer diagnosis.
Having been given a timeline on the wrong side of fair,
we sat in his dining room chairs and with a stare so full of love,
he said he was hungry and would love some grub.
With my shaking hands, I opened the fridge
and grabbed the Miracle Whip—
because he wasn't a mayo kind of man.
I remember with perfect clarity the clovers on his plates.
I traced those flowers to sedate my complete and abject misery.
It would be three weeks until he became nothing but a memory.
For those of you who have lost the most important person
in the world, know that this feeling is greater than any metaphor
or simile.
I won't compare his passing to a human tragedy
or environmental catastrophe.
I will not dishonour his memory by undercutting humanity.
He was just a man whose unconditional love shaped me.

I would wet his lips with a sponge in palliative care.
Always clean-shaven, he would have hated
his sprouting facial hair.
As a child, when he would groom,
I'd stand next to him in the bathroom and follow along
with the flat edge of the toothpaste tube.
At eighteen, I went away to university;
it was a natural part of my journey.
And at the age of eighty-seven, he got his first cellphone so that he
would never miss a call from me.

A Nokia brick he wore on his belt when it wasn't tucked away
on the shelf next to those same dining room chairs.
He once told me I was the only one who noticed
when he cut his hair.

Two days before he was gone, I had to go back to school.
I told him that I loved him and that I would see him again soon.
I squeezed his hand and kissed his cheek.
He had enough strength left to smile, though not enough to speak.
The cancer had made his lungs too weak.
Forty-eight hours later I got the call.
Thank God for the narrowness of my apartment hall.
Because with the words that stumbled out of my mother's mouth,
my knees gave out,
and the man who wrote the music to my song
was suddenly gone.

They saved his body so I could see him one last time.
On the bus home, my stomach was full of butterflies.
When they pulled him from that drawer and pulled back the sheet,
I recognized him from the mole on his cheek.
It was shocking to feel him so cold.
Until that moment, I had never ever considered him old.
And with an arm around my little sister, I once again squeezed
his hand and kissed his cheek.
And for the first time in my life I lost a piece of me,
to a man who baked cookies and never raised his hand.
A measure of masculinity my feminism completely understands.

There is a thread connecting our hearts,
two generations apart,
and through the Spirit World I can feel it tug,
to say he misses me, his little Becca Bug.
An angel in the heaven I desperately wish would exist,
though I don't hold out much hope.

But do I believe it was real for him and that helps me cope
with the scope of this loss.

You are a part of me.
In my eyes, my compassion, patience, and empathy.
In the tears that fall freely.
I will love you forever,
my hero,
my Grampy.

UNRESTRAINED LOVE

They restrain her
because she keeps tearing out her IVs.
They say, "Ma'am, please."
It doesn't matter how many babies she's delivered,
or that her blood disorder has all but destroyed her liver
and has worked its way into her brain.
She is a woman untamed.
Because of this fact, she is somehow to blame.

She's my mom.

She had a portion of her body removed and replaced
with titanium and steel.
You can feel the staples down her side.
She nearly bled to death the first time.
They restrain her; cuff her hands at her side because she is being
"difficult."
This woman, one of a handful from her medical class,
intelligent, bold, and brash,
once passed chemistry after pulling an all-nighter.
The police now question my stepdad, her full-time care provider,
about the bruises on her arms from where he'd catch her
when the seizures made her fall.
Where he'd grabbed her wrist before she hit the wall
or tumbled down the stairs.
Officers won't let him near her.
Question how much he cares.
But he knows when she's left alone she gets scared, so he's patient.

He buys a cup of coffee because he needs something to hold,
throws out the one he's bought for her because
it's now grown cold.
He takes her home and lays her down in bed,
wipes her tears with toilet paper because
he never buys tissues,
soothes her to sleep with talk of all their big plans,
not sure if she hears him or understands.
But when it comes to her,
he doesn't mind being tied down.

As My Mother Rolls Her Eyes

My hands have garnered a lot of attention.
From the length of my fingers and their unfulfilled
instrumental potential.
Their capacity to sprawl a piano's keys or guitar strings.
Their ability to stay soft in conflict.
The shape of their nails and the generations they hold.
How reaching out for comfort is considered bold
where I come from.
The scars on my knuckles are a gentle reminder that my skin
is the sum of two parts.
Freckled and teasing.
Identity pleasing.
That I'm closest to the bloodline that conquered the other.
I've always been just like my mother
in both demeanour and ambition.
Teeth pulled into straight lines.
But my smile betrays my audacity.
As though force could make anyone perfect.

I Hold Her in My Hands

She had a particular way of knitting her fingers together
while she waited for her nail polish to dry.
I was forever curious as to why symmetry didn't apply.
The nail on her index finger was rounded while
the nail on her ring finger was square.
Each stroke of polish applied with care.
There were ridges on her nails and mine were so smooth.
"It's something that aging will do," she'd say.
"Just wait, it'll happen to you too."
She never wore rings.
Never a wedding band or for fashion;
they would catch on the gloves needed for her profession.

Knuckles bumpy and bulbous
with delicate connections between each joint.

With each passing year, she lost more words
and my vocabulary grew.
And I knew she wasn't the same.
She became smaller and I garnered more fame.
Too busy to take a plane to see her.

Intellect replaced with aphasia and wails.
She can no longer sit still for her nails.

As I paint mine, I am careful around the square edges
of my ring finger.
I knit my hands together while they dry,
interconnecting my swollen joints.
It's difficult to remove my wedding band at some points of the day.
Frustrated that the nail polish won't lay flat on the uneven ridges
of my keratin.
Angry her illness was something as simple as
an unmeasured increase in ferritin.

It has been years since we've spoken,
our relationship corroded from rust.
I am my mother's daughter,
I've come to trust and understand.
And as I age, I take great comfort that I can hold onto her
in my hands.

Love Is

Love is hardest thing that we do.
We eschew all rationality,
reaching for a heart's embrace that many times ends up tragic.
Love's timing is rarely on point.
It's pain and pleasure,
two sides of the same coin,
and my pockets are full from the twenty I've broken.
I've got change to spare,
range to care,
words to share.
I've lived a thousand "what ifs" in the instant of a stare,
breath caught between the beats of a heart.
Love refuses to be dictated by rules for when to end
and when to start.
A thin societal veneer that tricks us into believing relationships are
linear instead of a scatter bomb.
And the beauty that blooms in the resulting chaos.

Love doesn't care if you're a good person.
It twists the knife.
Makes nice with your heart and riles up your head.
It embeds its tendrils in your bones, replacing veins.
Love isn't picky, it's fuelled by lust and anguish and pain.
Love wraps caterpillars in their cocoons,
plants them to sprout wings in your gut's womb.
It comes a little too late,
or a little too soon.
Loves takes and hides all of your spoons.

It lifts you up
and ties together your shoes,
so the smallest nudge makes you trip and fall.
Love is the trickiest trickster of them all.

More ostentatious than Crow,
sneakier than Coyote.
It chooses where it wants to go,
and goes there boldly.

Love takes without asking.
It bathes in your saliva,
leaving you dry-mouthed and tongue-tied.
And rides the shaky fists dangling at your sides.
Love devours your pride.
It implies great things.
Love infects your bloodstream.
But love is not always contagious, it would seem.

It manifests itself through lingering hugs,
nails drug across sweaty skin,
playful reactions,
acts of compassion,
and take-backs that aren't rationed.
It's expressed in spades or in fractions.
It's misplaced passions.
Love is the fine art of inaction.

Love is a serial offender.
It kills you while keeping you alive.
It vilifies compromise.
It spies your Achilles heel and attacks.
It makes you love someone who doesn't love you back.

Love fills pages upon pages of your writing pad.
Love has no confines or life hack.
Love is a paradox unabashed.
And love,
love is mourning the loss
of something you never really had.

Love Letter
to Confession

For you, I'll stay.
I'll let you pick and play your song on my heartstrings and pray
that you never forget the words.

I remember when we first met.
We bonded over late nights in your car as we watched the stars,
radio playing, saying the things we needed to say but couldn't
to just anyone.
Like how you needed to feel like someone cared,
just for you,
but you were scared to.
Your spirit was black and blue because vulnerability makes for
an easy target.
And in that car,
I didn't have to hide the scars because your trust was infectious.
We connected over what wrecked us on the day-to-day battlefield
of the big-kid playground.
We were high-school soldiers with an aptitude for helping
each other stand after being beat down.
Your eyes look at me in a way that say I am okay as is,
no need for plastics.
That my wit is biting and sarcastic,
just the way you like it.
That my ambition doesn't detract from it.
And by it, I mean our connection.
Formed over years of being misfits and rejection.

Mutual protection.
On the day we exchanged the keys to our hearts,
we began our start.

And yet I betrayed you.
I didn't stay true.
When after I had a few, I tripped and from my pedestal
I fell,
and gave another man access to my shell.
But never the heart within!
Because it's not there.
It's tucked away in your stare.
It's hidden between your fingers when you run them
through my hair
and the length of me.
And the care you take to hold me when panic shakes me
to my core.
Those are the places where my heart is stored.

Poor though I am in credibility,
I'm working towards stability.
An ability you would appear to have mastered,
while the walls of my soul flake like peeling plaster.
Your hands fit my chest.
Not just the way they touch my breasts,
but because they rest over my spirit,
and near it, you smile.
Something I haven't seen in a while,
because your cracked heart didn't see it as worthwhile.
I put your trust on trial,
sentenced it to death.
So I could feel another man's breath on my cheek
as your confidence leaks from our foundation,
poorly patched with overcompensation to make up for my
willpower's lack.

I know words are empty.
What I'm trying to say is, there will never come a day
when I won't need you with me,
even if it means walking a rope stretched tight across suspicion.
I'm exposing all of my vulnerability,
hoping your eyes see me and believe me,
that you can be the man I need so I can refine my stability.
In spite of the scarlet As on my chest,
just under the place where your hands are pressed.

Because I Have To

I'm pretty great, but I cry a lot.
And I've been told that I speak too much, that I talk a lot.
So I tend to overthink things and seethe a lot.
I take deep breaths a lot.
Walk a lot.
Tweet, 'gram, write, and push back a lot.
I cry.
A lot.
I get told to stay in my lane more often than not.
I can't help that I don't and won't fit in a box.
I was never allowed to call all the shots.
But I can build skyscrapers when given only half the blocks.
I've written Ph.D. dissertations and lectured at the school
of hard knocks.
I've torn through time and worked until thirteen o'clock.
Because I've had to.

I grew up without grandmothers to fuss.
I had a mother who worked too much to show her love.
I had a sister who hit more than she hugged.
My auntie was battle-worn and rough.
I learned that being a woman was about being tough.
So I pushed down my feelings and hid my thoughts.
Because I've had to.

I read a lot.
I consume books and articles.
I scrutinize font.
I will never be a jingle-dress debutante.

Red tape trims my shawl and ties my mocs.
My dance arena is city sidewalks.
I stand on guard for Elders to remember what they forgot.
So instead I took up the political front.
Waded through the academic and legal swamp.
I've replaced all my ancient words
with grades given on a bell curve.
A series of issued numbers legitimized my state.
My Creation Stories came from cassette tapes.
From a parent trying to escape his colonized fate.
I had written off my culture as a total loss.
Because I had to.

I forgive a lot.
I've let people take comfort at my cost.
Given up pieces of myself for them to accost.
This country I have criss-crossed,
running on fumes and emotional exhaust.
Did them a favour.
Gave them my labour.
Held the hands of haters.
Told them that with enough time, they'd get there.
I've made circles out of squares.
Because I had to.

I have a tendency to care.
I will sincerely accept your despair.
Clumsily stumble through smudgings and prayers.
Learning what was taken,
braiding my hair.
I will answer your emails and questions.
I will reply to your Instagram message.
I will gently accept and offer corrections.
Expand my understanding of culture definitions.
Fight for the angry and for the victims.

I will remember their names,
smuggle in keys to unlock their cage.
Accept that it's scary to be brave.
I will do all I can to protect and save.

I will mispronounce words I'm trying to learn.
I will speak just as loudly even when I'm not heard.
I will fight for a community that doesn't always accept me,
and that's fine because I'm working on my humility.
I will take up space.
Not because I always want to.
Because I have to.

I'M FINDING MY TALK

I'm finding my talk.
The one I never had.
The one that the schools took away from my dad.

I'm finding my talk
one word at a time.
Kwe
Wela'lin
Nmultes
Sometimes they are very old.
Sometimes they rhyme.

I'm finding my talk
when I'm up on the stage
telling big stories
or scribbling words on a page.

I'm finding my talk.
I'm meeting my family.
I'm making new friends
who choose to love me.

I'm finding my talk
with clumsy feet
that pat down the grass
with every drumbeat.

I'm finding my talk
with every bead.
My regalia speaks
through each stitch and seam.

I'm finding my talk.
It's in my smudge bowl,
when the smoke curls around me
and makes me whole.

I'm finding my talk,
how it's written across the land,
learning to take only what I need.
Netukulimk helps me understand.

I'm finding my talk
through my community.
From Elders to kids,
this world is still new to me.

I'm finding my talk
by speaking to my father,
by loving him,
by being his daughter.

I'm finding my talk
by speaking with my sister,
knowing we're different,
and I miss her.

I'm finding my talk
through my nephews and nieces,
teaching them they are complete
with all their different pieces.

I'm finding my talk,
it's on the inside.
It's how I see the world,
through not one, but two eyes.

I'm finding my talk
and it may take some time,
but I'm learning to speak
in a language that's mine.

KeSA'LUL

("I hurt you")

I Wish I Was Better at Writing Love Poems

I wish I was better at writing love poems.
I wish I was better at describing how my heart
is pinned to my sleeve.
How the angle makes it more exposed,
and how readily it bleeds.
How it needs to be comforted and reigned in
when I feel too much.
How it yearns for an honest touch.
How entangled it becomes with my other feelings
of anguish, anger, and lust.
I have all the words in the world to describe my rage,
when at a tender age I actually believed the history of my people
as it was written on the page, laid out for my consumption
with the assumption that my ancestral kin
are somehow unlinked to my light brown skin or their scars
that I carry within.

To this day, I still feel foolish for thinking I broke the mould.
That I was brave and bold.
When instead my spirit was sold to a tourist from a craft shop to hang
from their rear-view mirror as a trinket.
It's easier to pen angry lyrics than to admit
that I have to give colonialism a little credit.
Because 50 percent of the time my 50-percent bloodline
feels assimilated.

I haven't come to terms with the fact that my mixed heritage has
treaties of self-hatred negotiated.
When one bloodline tried its best to have the other annihilated.

I wish I was better at writing love poems.
Because I don't know how to hold beauty without criticism
or honour love without cynicism.
Forever looking for the witticism that underscores my recidivism
back into the status quo.
I can't forgive myself for what I don't know.
So instead I waste ink when I think of my self-doubt and pain.
Because a man with nothing to gain, whose Nation we call
the same, had the audacity to lay blame for my tongue's lack of
mastery in a language that I was never taught but that I have
fought for.
And I have bottomless syntax for the tears that fell,
much to his satisfaction, I'm certain.
I don't know how to eloquently translate this burden.
My kind writings are smudged on the page the way my sage
smudges a fake so I can say I'm authentic with my band number
and card as the hard line to my legitimacy.
Labelled with a community I've never lived in.

I wish I was better at writing love poems.
So that I don't have to justify why I belong.
So that I can have something beautiful to reflect upon.

I wish I was better at writing love poems.
Because with my new-found ability,
I would create the most heartfelt poetry.
If I had that capability,
the first poem I would dedicate to every part
of me.

FOOTNOTES

Introduction:
The following stories deal with mature subject matter
that may be disturbing.
It's a story about kids whose legacy is deserving
of something better than the vetted letter sent home,
lies in cursive promising they weren't so alone.
This story is raw.
It only includes what we saw.
But don't worry, there's hope.
Just scroll down to the footnotes.

Chapter 1: The Boats
Let's fast-forward through this part.
A bunch of men thought they could get a new start.
They came to Turtle Island with great intentions
to make names for themselves, never stopping to question
why we died from all their infections.

Chapters 2–6: More and More of the Same Old Shit
They thought they we better than us,
and we had no power to say enough is enough.

Chapter 7: All Indians Must Go to Heaven
Here we're going to take some time,
really delve into the divine.
The intentions of those who took our children,
the ones who said everything about them was forbidden.
It is in this chapter we will spill some serious ink,
because it is here we need to shift how you think.

Grown men, the future faces of our money,
felt like they had some problems;
they devised a national plan
targeting children to solve them.

Chapter 8: An Exercise in Faith
At this point, Canada is all in.
We're not trying to trash anyone's religion,
but the country chose to disregard our spirituality.
The Crown's rules, beliefs, and disdain was our new reality.
Pick a denomination,
just be sure to pick the correct one.

Chapter 9: So Many Lost Lives
The kids who went in
were erased by a system.
They lost the spirit under their skin.
Many disappeared,
their absence met with tears
as police or nuns or no one at all confirmed parental fears.

Footnote 1 for scope: Chanie Wenjack's Last Hope
A boy ran away.
Was given matches instead of a place to stay.
Found unmoving and cold.
He never got the chance to grow old.

Chapter 10: We Pick Up Our Pens

Footnote 2:
Storytelling is something we do.
But we decided that your style would be the best way
to get through to you.

Resume chapter.

We begin with unending resilience and laughter.
Survivors dictate their stories to those willing to listen.
Their voices a gift in addition to all they've already given.
The leader apologizes.
Our resolve finalizes.

Chapter 11: A Fallen Rock Star Becomes Our Secret Weapon
Cherished by the masses for his skilled verses.
Dedicated his last breath to our purpose.

Footnote 3:
He refused to let the world forget Chanie.
Though not everyone agrees with your legacy, I must say, Wela'lin.
Please rest peacefully.

Chapter 12: We Will Not Be Shelved
Determined to be heard,
we push back with protests, ceremony, love, and poetic verse.
This part is new,
settlers didn't rehearse.
We help them along, showing them it's baby steps first.

Footnote 4:
We will show them patience. Give them an opportunity to do more.
But make no mistake:
we will never go back to the way you treated us before.

Epilogue:
This section is currently being written.
It comes at your end,
but for us, it marks the beginning.

North America Rehashes Her Dating History With the Discoverers

Hi,
my name is North.
North America.
I'm a few billion years old, but who's counting?
We've all had some shitty relationships,
Amiright?!
I'm pretty independent.
I had great friends who were into what I had to offer.
I know I can be a bit rocky in places,
some of my spaces lack any kind of curve,
but expectations of perfection are a bit absurd!
And I'll admit that there are a few salty sides to my personality.
But geez, some men like to think that they should get all the credit
for your "discovery."

My first boyfriend was named Chris.
Total dick.
He would insist on giving nicknames to my friends;
he kept calling them Indians.

And even though they insisted they had different names,
this jerk said that they all looked the same.
He was one of those dudes with too much pride—
couldn't abide by any advice—
with the worst sense of direction.
When my friends politely tried to correct him,
he gave them a bunch of sexually transmitted infections!
I can't believe I swiped right for guy who people still think
deserves some kind of attention.
But between us girls,
he had the most underwhelming erections.

So when I dumped Chris, he was pissed, but I couldn't resist
this new guy named Giovanni—he went by John.
He liked my wilder side and didn't care if I "mowed the lawn."
But by dawn I could see he'd played me:
landed in my friends' neighbourhood, Mi'kma'ki,
established a fishing industry,
then left to go back out to sea!
He was one of those guys that when you had a party,
he'd invite all his friends.
Peace out.
And now I have a new roommate named England?
He keeps mooching off my resources, saying he's going to pay rent,
but geez, it's been forever and I haven't seen a single red cent!

I was tired of these Anglos and Italians,
all they did was bitch and complain.
So I was alone for a few years until a met this total dreamboat,
Champlain.
I have a lot of personal pain from guys I've let in before.
Well, let's be honest, less let in and more broke down my door.
So I got to see how this guy treated my friends.
It was refreshing to see a man do right and try to make amends.
Wait.

What!?
Not all of them!?
Dammit, Sam!
Stop instigating fights and picking sides.
I know I implied you weren't a bad guy,
that you and my friends were equal,
but when you murder the neighbours,
I think it's time we start seeing other people.

I've realized that I don't need a man to take care of me,
but I've been left needing some serious therapy.
My veins are shot.
All of my fish have been caught.
My friends hardly come around;
they've been evicted from their grounds
and stick to their own parts of town.
Some lady said they had to, "by order of the Crown."
Now, I'm left with scars on my face and oily blemishes
that continue to grow.
While some fuckboy and cheeto say they now run me.
But from what I can see, it's nothing but a peacock show.

I was so beautiful in my youth.
I might have been a bit less fancy,
but I knew I was aging gracefully.
Maybe for my next partner,
I'll try one of those new dating sites.
Put together a good profile,
only selfies in the best light!
Let me Google the top results where I'll meet the true love of my life.
Are you fucking kidding me?!
They're called Plenty of Fish and eHarmony?
Yes, I'm fine.
I swear I'll stop crying when I've dealt with the irony.

CREATURE CANADA

Today I'm going to tell you a Creation Story.

Many of you have heard them before, or at the very least have heard of them. We tell stories to pass on our knowledge and morals, and to teach lessons. This story is going to be a bit different than any story you might have heard before. It's not about Crow or Coyote, Bear or Klu'skap. It's a new story with old roots that cannot be appropriated.

Long before time immemorial, when there were only the plants, animals, spirits, magical creatures, and the original people who roamed this land, there was peace. Yes, sometimes people did not get along, but there was a consensus of how things were and would always be. There was a balance between Mother Earth and us, her children. The animals gave what they could and we honoured them for their sacrifice. We never picked the first plant, nor the second. We would only begin to pick the third plant, so that we would never pick the last ones.

We lived like this for more generations than you could count on all the fingers of your family.

Then one day a new creature came to our shores. At first, this creature was small, hidden. We didn't even know it existed. It came tucked away in the minds of the white man. Finding shelter in the intentions of those who brought it. At first, it did not have much power. It did not have a voice, only an inkling of a presence, and we were strong. We kept it a bay. We kept it subdued.

But the creature wasn't the only thing the white man brought. On his clothes, in his sweat, laced in his warm exhales, was something deadly. Sickness. The diseases burned through our people at an alarming rate. No man, woman, or child could escape the illnesses. As we began to die, the creature grew stronger. For the first time, the creature could speak. It whispered into the ears of the newcomers. Influenced their actions. With each task completed, the creature grew stronger, more powerful. It consumed our despair until it took shape.

Once it took on a form, its hunger could not be sated. Its endless greed consumed all the trees, hunted the animals, and fished the rivers until they only knew scarcity. It cracked open the body of Mother Earth and bled her black veins. Choked out Father Sky with smoke. It always picked the first plant. Every time.

The original people were helpless against its will. This creature cared not for our hearts and spirits because we were nothing but a problem. So it tried to control us. It confined us to the tiniest portions of our land. It rewarded those who would do its bidding with medals of valour and statues. This creature fed on the languages of our children. Separated families to weaken us. It thrived, nameless, until a dozen generations ago when it was finally given a name.

Canada.

Canada's skin was made up of laws. It had sharp claws that raked schisms into our communities so we would fight ourselves. We began to do Canada's work for it. We shamed our people, we kept ourselves under control out of fear for what Canada might do to us. We had heroes that took on Canada, but they were often punished harshly. Some of us tried to run away, only to discover Canada was vast and cold. They returned to the arms of Mother Earth. Sadly, there were some of us who gave up the fight. Canada tricked many of our people into believing it was right.

But in the smallest of places, our flame still burned on.

At first, resistance was small. Children whispered their languages out of earshot of Canada in the corners of the schools. We met in secret to share our stories and pass down our Elders' knowledge. We learned from each other. People who once warred were allies exchanging dance and song, but always cautiously.

But then one day, unexpected to Canada, the people who brought it to this land started to see Canada for what it was. You see, Canada was only as strong as the people allowed it. Its power was drawn from the hearts and minds of those who believed in it. It became what it was because it only fed on hate, fear, and prejudice.

Creature Canada, as strong and powerful as it was, had a weakness. It was blind. Canada couldn't see another world. It could only see what it thought the world should look like. It could not see what we did behind its back. It could not see peripherally. Though it was strong, the strongest foe the first people had ever met, because it had no vision, we were able to resist and persist. We created defenses. We wrote them down together, the original people and the newcomers. They were promises to each other that would live on generation to generation.

These promises still exist, and are used to keep Canada in check. Though it might try break these bonds, as long as we are still breathing, they cannot be undone.

Today, Canada is alive and well. It continues to pull power from the broken body of Mother Earth. It continues to feed off our spirits through neglect and hopelessness. But all is not lost. Because it is blind, it can be led to where we want to take it.

As we navigate these sidewalks of concrete, pass building of steel,
they've shaken out the earth from our hearts to mix the cement,
demanding we yield to progress.
We have been called "history" and "relics" for losing our roots,
that we replace our moccasins with that Nike swoosh.
But those observations are coming from you,
so full of yourselves that you're blind to our truths.
We keep beads in our pockets,
dropping handfuls from time to time
to roll back into the cracks of the streets with which
we are still so entwined.
We stand with our fish-scale eyes reflecting resilience
to those who look to us, refusing to be broken.
Our spirits have awoken from their colonized hibernation.
Your skyscrapers are tall but static, they've stopped climbing.
They've got nothing on us because we are still rising.
The story is not over.
Will you help us write the ending?

I am Honoured

My name is Swift Fox. Proud member of the Mi'kmaq Nation
of Mi'kma'ki.
The Wabanaki, People of the Dawn, with a legacy
twelve thousand years long.
And I am honoured.
I am honoured with overpriced beer and shitty hot dogs.
By juiced-up ball players and abusive running backs.
By packs of fans, packed into stands doing the tomahawk chop.

In 2013 a Philadelphia Eagles fan was photographed.
Impaled on his staff, crass and crude,
was a bust of an Indigenous man
and I was honoured.
In his grasp, a perfect pictorial of postmodern
cultural appropriation and genocide.
The public perception made perfectly clear:
the head of a dead Indian in one hand and in the other, a beer.

Daughter of a survivor and keeper of my family's culture,
I listen to my Elders and I know my teachings, my beliefs.
I stand tall against the culture thiefs.
And time and time again, I am told our leadership is not
being disrespected by the KC Chiefs
because I am honoured.

We are just caricatures,
mascots to amuse you.
Like the realest Indian on the block, Chief Wahoo.

Ancient mythical creatures entombed in lieu of respect,
our confidence wrecked,
bisected between public scrutiny and judgment
of too much sensitivity and contempt
for perceived easy corruptibility and so
I am honoured.

I'm saving my favourite for last,
the epitome of my righteous Indigenous wrath:
the Washington professional football team[1],
whose name is the IV morphine to the politically correct
beaten and battered ignorant majority.
A team name that is such an obvious racial slur.
A team name that, you'll have to concur, is literally colour-blind.
Because when it's all done and said, I'm really more brown
than I've ever been red.
A team name that alienates, isolates, racially perpetuates
our inferior status.
Whose trademark no longer has basis,
because even American copyright officers know that it's racist.
A team name that views us all with a narrowed-minded sameness.
A team name that will never pass these lips
or cross this cutting tongue
except to cut its supporters down by several rungs
because I am honoured.

I am honoured by eagle feathers that were given to me
upon the completion of my master's degree.
I am honoured by the hysterical laughter of my nephew
sitting on my knee.
I am honoured by my father's fifteen years of sobriety.
By a national inquiry and the right to marry a non-Native man
without the world questioning my indigeneity.

But I am just one person, so:

Take me out to the ball game,
take me out to the crowd.
I want my cultural pride back
but the world won't cut me some slack.
And it's rigged, rigged, rigged for the home team,
and know we're always to blame.
Because it's privilege that makes all the rules
in the honour game.

Redface

I've got a good one:
Johnny Depp, Rooney Mara, and a Cleveland Indians fan
walk into a bar.
Just kidding!
It's not funny.
Redface.
Let's just call it misplaced cultural appreciation
instead of blatantly obvious racism.
Criticisms of sensitivity are severe,
so I've decided to turn it on its ear!
This year for Halloween—wait for it,
it will score some serious points in the party scene—
I'm going to honour my ancestry
and go as my great-great grandmother,
a genuine full-blooded Caucasian princess.
But not to excess.
Just a tasteful amount of Starbucks Pumpkin Spice,
a messy topknot, and a Navajo-inspired Urban Outfitters dress!
I've accessorized it with Coachella tickets!
But no headdress;
I know that's racist.
I read *Huffington Post* in excess.
Are you offended yet?
Let's make it all better with a Twitter apology,
clasped-hands emoji, and the hashtag
#blessed.
By now,
I bet you're miffed.
You should be.
What I did wasn't cool.

So let me school you in your misplaced anger
at the frustrated Native instead of the warpaint wearer.
See, we lived through centuries of genocidal terror.
Catastrophic errors from simply being born brown in
the legacy of the Crown.
You? You doubled down on your privilege when you demanded
to see our cards,
inflicted and reopened generations of scars because you were
called out for the racist garb on your face.
Even poorer taste given the main act on stage.
Do you think A Tribe Called Red
are just a couple of Indians in a phase?
On some sort of display?
The few who broke free of the colonial cage?
Can you see why I'm enraged?
It's a shame that you chose the poet laureate to engage.
Because I don't pull punches when I play this game.

Our women go missing.
Our men shot and killed when they seek help
for a tire's de-rimming.
GoFundMe pages paint the shooter as the victim.
His story prioritized when accounts are conflicting.
Did you know we've never had an L'nu hold
the INAC minister's position?
So, on the inside,
my war paint is dripping,
pooling into my spirit.
I'm sipping the fire.
I am the physical embodiment in contrast of "Native-inspired."
I will not tread lightly.
I came armed to fight, you see.
Two degrees and enough community backing.

I will line up with my brothers and sisters to send you packing.
Because we are done with your attacking.
This is Turtle Island.
After centuries of being repressed,
you owe us a debt.
You can go wash your face now
and pay us your respects.

Matoax

It was all a lie.
I was appropriated as Disney's racist alibi.
They plucked me as a girl out of history,
and without ever mentioning my tribe,
they made me into a woman whose only worth
was to keep John Smith alive—
an event that was completely contrived.
It was all a lie.

All the while Jamestown and the Crown,
they converted my kin to cover their sin.
They made the world believe in
pilgrims, patriots, and heathens,
and I was left to make the leaves spin
with my whitewashed skin,
my people left to paint a future with the bleached-out
colours of the wind.

In order to protect me,
my community kept my real name shrouded in secrecy.
In your fairy tale,
I went from preteen to eighteen to baptism and Christianity,
all while my people continued to bleed.

Nobody knows that my name is Matoax,
but we all know the stories of blankets and smallpox.
They love our style, "Native-inspired," they rock our mocs,
using feathers for props, buying Urban Outfitters smudge kits
for fifty dollars a pop.

But there, your interest stops.
No one asks about the Highway of Tears,
the hunger walks.
Racial Integrity Laws? Nobody balks. Because everyone knows,
if you want to be an Indian princess, forget the culture that needs
to be sought,
just spit in a tube and mail it off,
tying an unlived identity to a single drop.

Did you know that I was kidnapped and held at a ransom
for swords and guns,
while my people were given booze and were racially shunned?
I had a daughter, a life—
I was married to Kocuom!
Something my full-length feature film decided was too much
of a plot conundrum, so they had him killed off
and made no mention of my abduction.

My sequel had me ditch Smith for Rolfe in holy matrimony.
That other husband?
A pop culture memory, just a savage phony.
This marriage counted,
by the grace of God and all His glory.
It is here that at least some good came of my story.

I never spoke about my feelings for Rolfe,
though they say he loved me so.
Our union brought peace to my people, and to his
literal boatloads of money from stolen fields of tobacco.
And so,
the spin given in England
was that I was the perfectly civilized Indian,
who could hand over your perception of a kingdom.
But behind your back, my jingle dress is jingling.

On my way home, I died from pneumonia or pox or tuberculosis,
and sadly, my history learned via osmosis
by frat girls in redface striking Native poses.
The bones of my people are buried in America's closet;
mine are just a bonus.
So many holes,
your lessons are built on history's osteoporosis.

The reality is this:
The English only wanted to flaunt us.
Their history continues to abuse and haunt us.
You don't even know my real name.
You only know me as Pocahontas.

Pennies

She slays with those double braids.
She is slayed because of those double braids.
The original voice silenced from those double braids.
They can be bought and sold, those double braids.
In fact, there's a sale at the Bay.
Look for the HBC original canoe
for your half-off Canadian-branded series of snowshoes.
Erase the creators of those goods.
Their origin and history need to be understood.
And use them for your favourite winter activities,
like lightly frolicking over her forgotten snow-covered body.
It's buy-one-get-one misrepresentations of her story.
Just look for the nearest store occupying our territory.
Check the back of your status cards for the special pin
to activate the coupon that includes free judgment to go along
with the perceived sin:
that what she got, she had coming.
And if she goes missing,
have her family bring in the newspaper clipping.
Show it at the register for discounted black suits, dresses,
and other dark labels.
Quality purchases that can be worn over and over again
as a funeral staple.
Given the societal climate,
they'll get plenty of wear out of this product.
Like last year's fashion, it's so easy to forget her.
Just toss her remains in Manitoba's aptly named Red River.
The vitriol comes free with purchase,
if she had some form of mental illness.

It's a points card full of expert witness
who would be remiss
if he didn't remind us she was at risk
because she chose to be in the sex-work or addictions business.
You'll find the apathy on the shelf next to the sacred
festival headdress.
After every ten biased news stories,
you get a free personal allegory
about a guy who knows a guy who dated a Native girl
because he doesn't see colour
and is well-read,
who wants a special gold star because he went to a powwow once
and totally listens to A Tribe Called Red.

I'd say their names but there are far too many.
We are the forgotten Canadian penny.
Our coppery skin removed from circulation over time,
because it isn't as valued as the lighter dimes.
It's ten for one—
what a deal!
Just like our land,
we come at a steal.

Her body's a commodity,
bought and sold as prepackaged Native spirituality.
Sorry, we don't sell an empowered Indigenous matriarchy,
but we do carry extra-exotified Indians (includes batteries).
And her life's receipt is marked Final Sale.
There are no refunds on colonization retail.
It's a Black Friday special with tax exemption.
It's our culture turned boho-style consumption.
Keep beating those drums for social redemption.
And maybe, just maybe, we'll get positive media attention.
APTN coverage of a Sunrise Ceremony on a red morning,

because the red are mourning the double braids found
ninety percent off
in the bargain box.
We don't know where they came from,
the tag was ripped off.

Intentions,
whether they pave to road to hell,
spell out your actions.
Are ignored instead of enacted.
Refracted realities, legal dualities.
Your intentions say a lot about you.
Like how treaties were signed, with no intended follow-through.
I wouldn't quite say he was a hero only because of his reluctance
to do so.
Perhaps a martyr.
A little rough around the edges.
In more than one or two ways, he transgressed.
He was but a man.
A Mi'kmaq.
Whose sacrifice can only be summed up by words I don't possess.
A man that the state, history, and colonialism made powerless.
Rose up, lifted by others, to confront those who would oppress.
He was stripped of his youth by a system
that, until he was seven, didn't recognize him as a citizen.
Because here's the thing.
When you know that your land, life, and treaty were all taken,
when there were schools that eradicated connections to your kin,
when you were only ever called an Indian,
you might find yourself in a position to rebel,
to take what little power you might have and excel at mischief.
But Marshall was convicted before the deal was even Sealed.[2]
No appeal existed for his existence as a disenfranchised
Indigenous youth,
whose delinquency for a structure that never fought for him
passed a conviction that required no proof.

That put a child behind bars for eleven years
and then acted aloof when confronted with another story.
Because at that time,
the shades of the teller went from caught living red-handed
to whitewashed allegory.
The case was closed.
No need to depose another witness to counter the whiteness
to fight this.
Because who would ever care about another drunk
or Native convict?
So much for the intended Peace and Friendship.

He tried to escape.
But unlike prison, the colonial legacy is still in good shape.
This isn't up for debate.
It quite obvious when a teen gets life for murder,
sentenced by perjure,
while the killer gets five for slaughter.
And yet, upon Ebsary's death, Marshall's father extended sympathy
to his family and daughter.
We might have generations of emotional baggage,
but Dan Paul was right: we were definitely not the savages.

If only this were the sole Crown bully in town.
I could drown in the ink spilled on his prejudiced rap sheet.
But I could swim in an ocean if there were a drop for every action
that broke treaty.
And I can feed my spirit with the resilience of my ancestry.
Marshall's life not only changed the evidentiary,
he gave us a chance to live the practices of another time.
A lifeline to the past,
where our lands were vast.
A moment where we were not defined by a band number next to
our face encased in plastic.

How fantastic a thought: we were people,
Nations.
From fishing eels
to Supreme Court cases to help us heal,
we couldn't help but feel hopeful.
The Marshall Decision.[3]
We could once again go back to our traditions for a living.
So we hit the water and started fishing.
But the affirmation didn't do much to combat
the deep-seated racism.
Our rights were affirmed but we were rejected.
It would appear that we weren't selected to be protected.
So we protested the people with hate and fear that had infected
their hearts.
The iron commitment had completely rusted away from when
we buried the hatchet.
Because a second decision snatched it.
Altered it.
Changed the implications.
Conservation was the justification.
But we are the First Nations.
We know that this land is not ours, but borrowed
from the seventh generation.

I began this poem by saying he wasn't a hero.
I stand by the writings of my pen.
Because I would suggest that instead, when Marshall died,
he did so as a legend.
His dedication to his people and his disdain for the Crown
resounds in our people today.
The reverence we have when we say his name will only grow
from story to myth.
About a man who had no intention
of putting down his fishing kit.

Pain in All Directions

I always had skinned knees,
scabs on my elbows.
I was bruised constantly.
Sometimes from climbing trees I was told were too tall.
And sometimes from a deliberate push designed to make me fall.
At school I was once asked about my black eye,
and I lied.
I was practiced and it was easy to dismiss
the fact that my sister sometimes solved her problems
with her fists.
My teachers would nod and say, "That's what siblings do,
but don't worry, you'll get her back one day soon."
Humming the same old "eye for an eye" tune.
You see,
nobody at my school understood
that my dad was doing the very best he could.
He kept his pain locked deep in his chest.
From the very moment he went from being smudged
to being blessed, his pain passed to my sister
and history took care of the rest.
It went from his spirit to her brain.
Her emotions could not be tamed.
From there, it didn't go very far;
it left its legacy on my body in stitches and scars.
But I kept a brave face.
My hurt was hidden in plain view.
I built barriers and walls.
Nobody ever knew.
It became my normal.
My endurance only grew.

Because I had no choice; I had other things to do.
I had to grow up in a world where my pain had no room.
But I was a dandelion:
given any chance, I would bloom.
I was the first to be cut down,
but the first to spring back.
I made a decision that I would never be the first to attack.
Because if I inflicted pain,
then the cycle remained the same.
All the way back to when the Church made my father forget
his real name.
For a people who passed down our stories with words,
never writing things down,
we never spoke of this pain, we never made a sound.
We didn't have a safe space.
We went from a beautiful culture to being displaced.
We had no choice but to simply survive.
We did all we could just to stay alive.
Fighting battles against depression, anxiety, and suicide.
Our children feel it from their muscles to their teeth,
from inside their spirit to the bottoms of their feet.
We try to ignore it,
as though it's an easy deflection,
but it's hard to fight pain that comes from all directions.

So, here's your gentle reminder that we are still here.
In spite of generational trauma and a culture of fear.
And we are getting better,
repairing our DNA,
caring for each tiny letter,
trying to rewrite our chapters
with an abundance of family, fry bread, and laughter.

The world might not be ready for us.
We avoid doctors and nurses because we were stripped
of our trust.
But we're bridging that gap.
It has to be a must.
Because our time of oppression is entering its dusk.
So we express ourselves through drums, dance, and art.
After all, pain and feeling are tied to the heart.
Our capacity for resilience
is nothing short of brilliance.
We are healing with purpose and building capacity.
We are growing back roots severed by tragedy.

My father ditched the bottle a long time ago.
And in my life, he now makes regular cameos.
My sister has unclenched her fist.
With her open palm,
she now blows me a kiss.
Instead of pain, I will pass love onto my kids.
And I will work to improve a biased system,
one our children can feel safe in.
We are asking to be given a chance to heal,
so that pain will no longer be the biggest thing we feel.

KE'SA'LUL

("I place you into the fire")

It's Your Turn

My voice might sound familiar,
delivering slivers of a truth you've never known.
My cadence might ring a bell,
I've got that lilting tone.
You've heard my words before.
Tiny marks on a page, it would seem,
marked by a blinking cursor or a cellphone screen.
Tapping out bars on a bus.
Scribbling passages of loss and lust.
Posting nothing but robust lines.
Redefining time.
Because I'm tired of you saying so
I'm coming through your radio,
rapping bars to tribal labels,
burning down all your fables,
riding the airwaves of mega-stage speakers.
Toppling statues, calling for justice
by the drum and by the steeple.
Carrying the lives of my people
in my pen.
Don't make me repeat myself again.

I wasn't always a poetry powerhouse.
I didn't always take on politicians,
speaking patiently over shouts.
In fact, I didn't always belong.
It was decades before I found the words
to my song.

Little baby L'nu,
eyes full of hope.
I had yet to be bruised;
I had plenty of rope.
Lacking in scope of the here and now,
the past and then.
I didn't know what it took to be an Indian—
let alone Mi'kmaw.
But my communities' resilience
was the most beautiful thing I ever saw.
I wanted to go there.
So I grew my hair,
wore all the beaded and leather flair,
because I had yet to understand
that it was the love of my nitaps that made the man.

I've taken some licks and make amends.
I broke my heart among many, had to grow thicker skin.
Paid in blood and tears for other people's sins.
Got dizzy from all the spin.
From protests signs to government red-tape lines.
Education and emancipation from others' expectations.
I'll put sovereignty and respect above any reputation—
including my own.
Because I just want to go home.

For you listening for the pithy ending,
that famous mic drop cleansing,
where my words are sending the message you want to hear
and a list of things to do.
Too bad.
For once, I'm going to leave all the work up to you.

Nothing Special

She will not be special.
There will be no reference to her "next level."
She will not break barriers or be the first.
Her success will not quench a guilty thirst.
Her history will not be both blessing and curse.
And she will only experience unexpected hurt.

She will walk on shards of glass as she stares at the sky.
There will be no broken-barrier high.
She will sigh, content in her place.
She will have no need to demand space.

She will be unremarkable simply by birth.
She will have normalized worth.
She will slip through streets unnoticed.
She will automatically be given an earnings bonus.
Her claims of pain will never be called bogus.
And her need to do so will be measured in iotas.

Invisibility at its finest.
Her smile will not be coaxed from shyness.
There will be no singular day of celebration.
There will be no challenges to her remuneration.
She will not be a ghost or host to ego.
No one will dissect her chromosomes,
debate the merits of her free throw.
No chants of "Wherever she goes, we go."
Banners about pussies and wit
will languish in the garbage pit.

There will be no protests of over body business
because no one will give a single shit.

Her existence will be seamless.
She will not do more and dream less.
She will banish the diminutive suffix.
She will be ignored and respected.
She will not be society reflected.
There will be no compliments that need to be deflected.

She will be left alone.
And finally, she will feel at home.

THIS THING CALLED THE ARTS BUSINESS

It is the creative process
for a product that opens more minds than it closes.
In order to teach and heal from my opus,
I'm parting the dissonance like Moses,
deciphering the rhymes that I've coded
to break free from what society has moulded.

I've opened up my scars for this.
I have re-broken my heart for this.
This thing you call the Arts Business.
With hopes it doesn't turn to shit.
It's music and melodic bliss.
It's all out there for a chance to miss.

I've scraped off all my callouses.
I have softened my protective edginess.
Woken up from my sleeplessness
to scribble down the words that itch.
Plucked strings,
the only cure for finger twitch.
Maintained a sense of openness.

For you all to poke and prod my head.
I've shown you just how much my memories bled.
I've taken you into my bed.

Broke open creative bread for your satisfaction
to share a meal made of my resilience and passion.
Hid all the pieces that are still in fractions.
Presented you with only the best of my ashes.
Made grand entertainment from the tragic.
I've turned my bruises into magic!

I've painted pictures out of words.
Made you connect to the absurd.
Made familiar what you've never heard.

I've built friends from this.
I've lost friends for this.
I've fallen into madness.
And buried my sadness.
In this thing you call the Arts Business.

I've gained knowledge and I've profited
from a history that never cited it.
Because it saw success and us as the opposite.
But I strung words from everything it closeted.
Stepped on stage and deposited.
A truth once trapped in my esophagus
is now presented with confidence.
And I have art to thank for this.

Jotted down on pages.
Made a priority in all its stages.
The writer's block.
The ticking clock.
The inspiration that doesn't stop.
The advancement of the plot.
The progress that's hard-fought.
The impending deadline.
The streamlined sublime.

We take back our power.
We create at every hour.
The page after page of utter crap.
The blistered fingers that start to crack.
The words spoken that we can't take back.

So we artists write our apologies down.
Find that perfect note and that resonating sound
to sum up how we truly feel.
Give lyrics and voice so that we and they can finally heal.

Because of art,
I can grandstand to a sea of whiteness
and leave behind all my politeness.

We do art in our solitude.
In groups, or as interlude.
We strive for those YouTube hits.
And those double clicks.
Hustled and sold tickets
to try and get ahead
in this thing called the Arts Business.

For good causes,
and political pauses,
we've given our spirits and souls.
Reaching out to the young and old.
Been on and broken benders
and confirmed our genders.

It has allowed me to breathe.
It has allowed me to grieve.

Because of art,
we've started to put back together what was torn apart
and present you all with something whole.
We've burned it all to the ground,
then rebuilt it into a home.
We have made priceless
this thing you call the Arts Business.

WHAT I LEARNED
FOR THE COST
OF AN EDUCATION

Thousands of dollars have been paid
so I can put four letters after my name.
As if my name, as is, is insufficient to be trusted;
it must be stuffed, plumped, and tufted with abstract ideas
encrusted on my brain.

BA. Bachelor of Arts.
As in, Be A sheep trained to bleat what the prof seeks for his pay.
MA. Master of Arts.
As in, I Am a person trained to think while letting the reality
of my life sink in.

So, what have I earned with all my years learned?
I can write good—
I mean well.
I can spell success without debt.
But those who owe their futures, a game of Russian roulette,
their payments forever set.

In Anatomy and Biology, I learned the topography of a cell.
My short stint in science taught me that reliance
on compliance and courtesy
is an insurgency on my urgency to be loved.

You see, receptors can be fooled and tricked.
Chemicals contradict the scripts to keep you safe.
A place once guarded now bombarded, a fall too far from grace.
Because in my desperation, I let him in.
To feel pretty, I bent to his whim.
My heart turned to tin as he explored the skin of another
because my request to be faithful all but smothered him.
If you ask me, he had a bit too much mothering.

Math taught me that correlation doesn't always equal cause.
For example, cancer and cure both start with a C
but that does not mean they are related.
And so,
my goodbye belated, my soul berated, because my new-found
hobbies of boozing and getting naked left me clueless that the
Creator was taking back what he had created.
And to this day, I'm ashamed of it.

Anthropology taught me that really, it's you and not me.
That pain runs deeply,
sometimes generationally.
That success doesn't come conveniently,
and that I can be loved so completely
even the hardest moments pass easily.

I learned nothing from Psych.
Not because I wasn't able;
it simply didn't fit in my timetable.
And I might be a little unstable;
I could spend hours picking myself apart.
Yet, in spite of never opening a textbook,
I consider myself an expert on matters of the heart.

You see,
sound thoughts need practice for the firing synapses,

an axis for the logic that knows he's gone.
But my hope, a star wished upon, waits for him to respond.
Sitting up there, watching from the clouds amongst the crowds,
and my heart is sated.
Because for nearly thirty years, he waited for his true love.
Whose health disease never discriminated,
her breasts were excavated,
tumours her lungs cultivated.
Needless to say, me and my grandmother never were acquainted.

Now, I'm not trying to knock a good education,
but everyone needs to unlearn the misinformation brought on
by societal placation.
And collecting letters after your name does not get you the keys
to the kingdom, poverty freedom, or a cultural anthem.
Your credibility is held at a degree's ransom.
No.
School provides a venue to gain perspective and be reflexive.
Gives you time to shift your paradigm and adjust your context.
While engaging in safe, consensual—and, let's all admit,
sometimes experimental—dorm-room sex.

What they teach you puts you in situ to change the game
in which you won your truths.
The ones you use to operate when you cooperate to exonerate
history.
Because if there is one thing we all love, it's consistency.

Learning is a process.
I don't know everything,
and what I haven't learned yet isn't my fault.
Which is precisely why
I store my degrees next to my salt.

Just Another Native Poet

Be sure to diversify your pieces.
You wouldn't want to be pigeonholed as a Native Poet.
So it was said to me and me to myself in my constant self-doubt
that after a while my passion for my people would fall
on deaf ears and rolled eyes.
The following, a taste of why I will never give in on hustling
my allies.
Every word is something I've witnessed, read, or heard.
So I ask that you listen before you tell me what I say is absurd.

Here we go again, they'll say to themselves.
She's probably going to talk about water quality and mental health.
Twenty years of boil orders and contaminated wells.
Or one hundred and forty attempts in two weeks to kill themselves.
It can't be THAT bad because I hear that if you live on reserve,
chief and council will give you a free house.
As a tax-paying citizen,
I don't believe we should continue to support them.
So what if we spend four thousand dollars less each year
on every one of their children,
because the young and white are the new post-secondary victims.
Affirmative action and designated seats are taking away
opportunity from the country's elite!
I worked hard to get where I am with no help from charity;
achievement should be based on a meritocracy.

Because the halls were full of people who looked like me,
I must have been outstanding to earn my degree.
I have never, ever been given something for free.
I can't even express my opinions on the CBC
because everyone is too concerned with being PC.

So you can see why my frustration can push me to the other side
of angry.
Just because you feel your experience payments are a little light
doesn't mean someone somewhere hasn't already paid the price.
History's voice is colour-coded
by those who have always had the right to vote for it.
Do you know what it's like to only see yourself appropriated?
To see Karlie Kloss wearing a headdress on the runway half naked?
To be told that spray-painted racial slurs on our homes
are incidents that are isolated?
You're lying to yourself if you think colonialism is outdated
because I need a government-issued card to prove that I'm Native.
A card that expires every ten years.
Point me to a colonizer whose ethnicity can be held in arrears.
I would like to read the federal White Act.
I'd like to see your equivalent to e-tags and a rez pass.
Maybe live in a city that was founded by a man who put a bounty
on your scalps?
On the corner of Cornwallis Street
is where our Friendship Centre is housed.

Did you ever stop and think why we are called redskins?
Maybe because we've spent generations trying to scrub off
the moniker of "dirty Indian."
Trudeau is great and all, but statistically
I am still five times more likely to go missing.
Justin, that Haida tattoo is cute
but you've got to sit down and listen:
It's time to get this country in a treaty condition.

You can all suck your teeth and roll your eyes but I'm simply
not ready to diversify my writing to go with it.
Because I'm am proud to be pigeonholed as a Native Poet.

Ancient Memories

We remember.
Back before farmers with guns.
Back before our women were worth less than our sons.
Back before trailer hitches and false accusations.
Back before hood life and reservations.

We remember.
Back before white papers.
Back before we were told we needed Christian saviours.
Back before we were considered the local exotic flavours.

We remember.
Back before they pulled plastic from this earth to issue cards.
Back before we wore tattoos of generational scars.

We remember what it was like.
Before our gatherings were deemed illegal.
Back when we negotiated treaties as equals.
Back before colonization created Great Britain's sequel.

We remember.
Back before we were branded with band numbers.
Back when our drums rang through the air like thunder.

We remember.
What it means to be a community.
We remember life lived in unity.
We remember in our bones.
We remember in our moccasin soles.

We remember in drum beats,
rhythmed feet, seed beads, tobacco leaves.
The simple fact that we will never leave our territories.
Because we make ancient memories.

We remember tomorrow and a thousand years ago,
from eel weirs to the buffalo.
We remember petroglyphs and Instagram photos.
See, we remember our history
without statues, money, or pictures of the queen.
But they tend to forget,
tweet out apologies:
280 characters of regret.
Only back to status quo, like the future is present.
But we're good people, us First Nations.
We'll hold out our hands for reconciliation.
So we will knock on Parliament's front doors.
And we will remind them that, like us,
they need to remember more.

Reconcile Your State of Mind

As a nation we have missed our mark by one hell of a mile.
For the history that defiled my father's culture when he was
just a child,
to the society that exoticizes our braided hairstyles,
to the public that buries their heads in the sand piles,
whose finger-pointing reviles our chiefs and beliefs
can breathe easy, because as of 2015,
we are reconciled.

Which means we're no longer judged, and a Dakota child
won't be sent home for the fact that he smudged because he found
his brother cold when touched.
And there is no grudge against the fact
that sometimes I get tax-free gas.
But only in pre-approved, monitored amounts—
I wouldn't want to be brash with the spending of my
government-given cash.

We have accepted the norm of more Natives in prison,
unable to forgive them for the traumas they've suffered,
content to maintain a buffer between reality and comfort.
Our biased history spun to finally deal with the
Indigenous conundrum.

And we have come to terms with the panic in my father's eyes
when he reads the apology of lies,

taking time to exorcize the demons that swirl in his soul,
the one that was saved and placed into the hole left by the loss
of his language.
But at least he's got $3,000 in education credits to sandwich
his time in lieu between now and the years he spent
in residential school.
Dad, I have been practising. Kesalul.

I'm sorry if this reference is so tensile.
I'm working my way through the stages of grief,
still so caught in denial that I nearly forgot!
We are reconciled.
The Highway of Tears? Girl, that was so last year.
No need to fear that you'll be snatched or attacked,
because it's a fact.
We are reconciled.

Now, may I be so bold as to make a suggestion?
Instead of a budget and a timeline for reconciliation,
how about an accurate portrayal of history in our
nation's education?
Bring back the National Aboriginal Health Organization?
Institute classes for language reclamation?
Question why there are so many Aboriginals incarcerated?
Or at least develop a strategy for suicide prevention because
we kill ourselves up to eleven times more often,
and if we had one, Dakota kids wouldn't have to see their
little brothers in coffins.
And to soften the line in the sand we all tend to draw,
and eliminate common words like "redskin" and "squaw."
I've washed my hands so many times they are raw,
but I can't shake the frustration that we are still referred to
as "Indians" under the law.

Worry not.
Take off my shoes;
no need to walk that mile.
Because Canada has spent enough money,
checked all the right boxes.
All of our accounts have been compiled,
our "perks" and "benefits" beguiled.
Congratulations, Canada,
you have finally reconciled this nation's state of mind
so that in the face of our suffering,
you will always turn a blind eye.

What Good Canadians Do

Are you a good Canadian?
Do you take great pride in the country we live in?
Do you explore the oceans, the prairies, and mountains?
Do you brag about your health care to all your foreign friends?
Change your cover photo to maple leaves and pride flags,
boasting inclusively?
High-five your diverse social group
while Molson Canadian toasting?
Do you give standing ovations for new Canadians
at their swearing in?
Do you clasp hands with Indigenous women and men?
Empathize with the struggles we experience?
Do you lend a hand to those you don't understand?
You identify with more than double doubles and hockey stadiums.
You would never use words like "squaw," "redskin," or "Indian."
Of course not, because you are a good Canadian.

This is a country that I want to be able to believe in;
it's land that has been in my family for a thousand generations.
You support us because you know we are equal citizens,
that we should remain kind in our united fight
against a biased system.
You listen to those who are different from you.
You are always willing to walk a mile in another person's shoes.
You are grateful that we are just the red and white, not the blue.

You've taken your history lessons as only one form of the truth
because you recognize and acknowledge that 150 is,
for some of us, relatively new.
Of course, because that's what good Canadians do.

You understand why some don't celebrate, so you won't get mad.
See, they cut out a maple leaf and laid the white square
over red territory,
they told us it wouldn't be so bad.
Then they raised our stolen lands to be flown as the Canadian flag.
So you respect that difference of opinion doesn't give you a right
to make me a comment-section punching bag.
After all, you celebrate diversity as an enduring Canadian trait,
and not a passing fad.
You will protect, at any cost, those who worship
at your neighbourhood mosque
because the safety you have today, so many have lost.
Your desire to reconcile is consistently renewed.
You believe Canada is more than a history of old white dudes.
And you know that a person's ethnicity amounts to more
than just food.
Because that is what good Canadians do!

You are honoured by our history of keeping the peace.
You love our environment and know that resource extraction
is not a renewable lease.
You understand that some of us are afraid of police.
So you offer to decode for those who don't understand the legalese.
You know that this country has room for millions more refugees.
You love that we have so much freedom of speech,
but that doesn't mean what you say is consequence-free.
After all, we own what we speak because we're Canadian, please.

We know we're not perfect and we own our mistakes.
We pledge to do better because we know what's at stake.
We will be good allies, and not insufferable flakes.
The marginalized are not for the privileged to dictate.
As a Native woman, my thoughts you appreciate.
And my missing sisters cause you much heartache.

The Canada of tomorrow will be better than Canada is now
because it's not about free concerts and being one in the crowd.
It's about applauding the fact that I am Mi'kmaq and proud.
You will leave here tonight and you will be better.
You will Google the names Colten Boushie, Tina Fontaine,
and Barbara Kentner, and you will realize what it means
to be called a settler.
You will be kind, respectful, and compassionate,
through and through,
to all of those who are different than you.
Because after all,
that is what good Canadians do.

LIVING TREATIES

They said they were irrelevant,
not worth the paper they were written on.
They were simply pawns to bond us to the monarchy,
to control the anarchy,
to establish a patriarchy and take away our unceded lands,
confine us to bands that were set aside and reserved.
The legality of those agreements was deferred,
preserved and archived,
but like us, they survived the passage of time
until they were once again spied by Mi'kmaw eyes.

Learning about our histories is long overdue.
Much like a refracted pebble in a pond,
the perspective has always been slightly askew.
What we believed to be crystal clear, an affirmation,
our best intentions,
to secure the future of the next seven generations,
was written down in a foreign language—
not our Native communication—
and thus, the intended meaning of our words was lost
in translation.

And therein lies the keystone of this cultural bridge:
there were treaties that were signed in peace and friendship,
but they were treaties that implied a Mi'kmaw stewardship,
a reciprocal relationship.
1752 needs to be annually revisited and reaffirmed to confirm that
we are the original inhabitants of this land,
our ancestral hood.

Because it's not just what was written on parchment,
but how it was meant to be understood.

The treaties still matter!
They are not simply smatterings of ink,
they are promises, words to make you think and take you
to the brink of your privilege.

Time after time, our treaties were denied,
and perhaps they could have died
if not for the individuals who took up the fight
to assert our Indigenous rights.

Grand Chief Gabriel Sylliboy[1] was not to be toyed with.
Armed with only his knowledge and poor English,
he took to the courts.
The reports say it didn't end well.
That as a savage, he was at a disadvantage when entering his plea.
But from what I know, I disagree.
He fought for what he believed.
I heard that when he spoke,
there was total silence.
His voice would move even the leaves on the trees.
He was the spark that ignited our fire.
Our cases we took to the courts,
higher and higher!

In 1982 the constitution recognized,
then made them into law in 1985.
See, we knew all along that Sylliboy committed no crime.
What he started set the stage for 1999:
enter Donald Marshall Junior.

DMJ took on the Crown twice.
The first time stole eleven years of his life.

Once again, a Mi'kmaw man was asserting his rights,
and Marshall became an unlikely hero to the treaty plight.
With his actions came the Marshall Decision—
but not without certain conditions.
Because we still live in a colonized world,
there was an unprecedented second decision,
a "clarification" and "elaboration,"[5]
but still, an historical occasion.

Because before him, it was a case-by-case basis.
And with each victory taken, the province preferred negotiations
to litigation.
They still continued on with intimidation.
And while they were hoping for Mi'kmaw pacification and
placation, we were beefing up Mi'kmaw education.
And once those floodgates were opened,
there was no stopping the Mi'kmaq Nation.
Because we understand there is no such thing as
Mi'kmaw standardization.
We quit playing games the moment Cornwallis signed
that proclamation.

Flashback to 1990 when the province retreated.
Before they began, they were completely defeated.
They walked straight out of the courtroom;
it had charged the wrong group of L'nus
for traditionally hunting some traditional food.
A little birdie informed them and told them they would lose,
that their argument was hollow.
(In fact it was a msikue'j,
otherwise known as a sparrow.)[6]

The treaties are still alive.
They continue to help us thrive.

They are built into our family dynamic.
They've imprinted themselves on our Native genetics.
They are prophetic in their aesthetic,
charismatic, democratic, and systematic,
but never meant to wreak havoc.
It isn't our fault that many of you find them so traumatic.

Most importantly of all,
they are not solely ours to rise up beyond
the level of equal.
You tend to forget,
two sides signed those sacred documents.
We are all treaty people.

Every day is National Indigenous Peoples Day

#WATERISLIFE

An Elder once told me,
if you don't step into the water, how will it feel your sincerity?
With perfect clarity, Grandmother Water knows the severity
of where we are at.
Because a simple shift in syntax has a dramatic impact.
From kin to resource and earth to shale,
there is a common misbelief that our future is somehow up for sale.

Stale promises of job creation and economies
have taken precedence over easy facts like, If you cut us, we bleed.
Politicians have planted seeds that have grown into a belief
that we are somehow above it.
That we are disconnected.
Unaffected.
Foolishly protected from consequence.
It is bottomless bank accounts that have trounced common sense.
And now my womb is lined with dollars and cents
instead of babies growing surrounded by water's presence.
I have been paid to believe that I can feed my children with
adequate financial compensation for environmental devastation.
And when I cry for the extinction of the salmon,
my tears will be reference pages for long-term
strategic-plan action.

Our lungs are made up of 83 percent liquid inspiration.
Our hearts beat with 73 percent of earth's perspiration.
And our blood is 92 percent in a dire situation.
So it is with 100 percent earnest invitation that I ask for a future
for the next seven generations.

The premier does not have a premium on treaty rights.
Us L'nus have never shied away from a fight,
and we will unite for this water, for us and for you.
Because even the greediest of men need water to live, too.
We want to make sure that you hear what we have to say.
Like Standing Rock and their tipis, we set up our eel weirs
prepared to stay.
I will not let this go, whether we live by the drum
or under the steeple.
Make no mistake, Mr. McNeil:
the Mi'kmaq are not a conquered people.
History might have temporarily colonized the land,
but give us time,
before you know it, we will have Indigenized your mind.
Introduced you to a little Two-Eyed Seeing instead of boasting.
Then, even the richest of men will realize they need water
for their champagne toasting.
How dare they sip on chilled H_2O in the courtroom,
or use water cannons to subdue those who refuse to stay idle?
They use the AC in winter months because they are in
climate change denial!
But the joke is on us.
Protecting the water is a must, can't you see?
Because the earth would fare a lot better without us, or humanity.
We are on a one-way street without an escape tactic,
just to fill our wallets with multicoloured pieces of plastic
that we can't eat, or use to keep warm.
A house made of twenties won't weather a storm.
Can you use that five-dollar bill to reverse a boil order?
Or a ten sheet to make our Arctic a little colder?
I would give up all the hundreds in the world so I could tell
my unborn daughter with comfort, "You'll understand
when you're older."
Instead of fear for what kind of future this land holds for her.

But it can all be reduced to bitter irony.
To poison a river for a paycheque must be a hell of a thrill,
just so that we can go home to pay the water bill.

The Talk

Hey, Canada.
I know you've been trying.
You're starting to own up to all the lying.
You're starting to see how hard we've been vying.

But the thing is,
many of us are still dying.
I know you feel bad about our missing women.
I know your heart breaks for our children,
the ones who were taken and the ones who live
in the foster care system.

You've certainly made an effort to get through to me.
I really appreciate that apology.
But you must put a bit more focus on accountability.

You can't just say you're sorry and not take the time to listen.
And you need to be patient while you wait to be forgiven.
Keep in mind so much of my family still have substandard
living conditions.
Think for a minute about what it must be like
to have never had tap water once in your life.
Please don't interrupt me, I'm not trying to make light.

I understand that there is so much on your plate,
what with trade, and war, and what's going down
in the United States.
I just want you to understand that our lives are still at stake.
There is no need to get defensive in this conversation.
We all need reminders of what we need to do for reconciliation.

You wrote that big report with the TRC,
but those 94 calls to action are just a bit of what we need.
I mean, people still dress up as me when they go out
for Halloween.
You did well in getting started,
you planted the right seeds.
But we need a lot more time, a spring after winter,
if we're to regrow our leaves.
Remember, we're just relearning how to breathe.
How to be free.
Just like our teachings, we could all use a little humility.
Might I suggest you take some time to read?
Have a look at the treaties.
I could even recommend a few great lines of poetry.
I don't want to scream and fight.
I don't want to point out all the times you forgot about our plight.
I don't want to get into how you thought what you were doing
was right.

Because at the end of the day, you were wrong.
You took our culture, our voice, our words, and our songs.

You made me feel ashamed for trying to live out a part of me.
You denied me my history.

But I bet you didn't know that we were so sneaky.
That we kept whispering in the dark when we were
supposed to be sleepy.
And that now we stand in government, schools, and universities.
Because in spite of your best efforts, we still occupy our territories.
I'm not trying to lay blame on your citizens specifically—
I know they weren't responsible for our situation personally—
but it's important for them to recognize they benefit
from our disparity.

Here's the thing I want you to take away:
we are really open to having you stay,
but we're going to have to make new rules by which we all can play.

No more telling me who I am.
You don't get to be mad just because you don't understand.

We also need to talk about your expectations
for how quickly we can actually heal from your exploitation.

Again, if you're serious about growing this relationship,
it's really important to the process for you to acknowledge
all your shit.
I'm not saying it's easy, but together we can get through this.
It's perfectly normal if you're feeling distraught.
Everyone stumbles when trying to learn
what they've never been taught.
Making amends is about moving forward,
but it's also about knowing when to stop.

For example:
If we could do something about these cards,
the ones you say we need to have but make access to far too hard
(let alone we're not the ones to issue them to start),
because you still want to identify us by a standard chart.

But it's not about you.
Or how much you think you do.
Or whether you think you've done enough to be through.

Because this talk is about us.
It about you earning back our trust.

So you can start by talking to your friends and family.
You know that racist uncle who keeps saying Indian
unapologetically?
And the ones who refuse to even acknowledge me?
The ones who tell me I'm so lucky
because mixed-race women are so damn pretty?
Calling them out would go a long way in helping me.
Because they don't want to listen or see what I see.
They think I want them begging on their knees.
Honestly, I just want some reciprocity.
You've given so little but have asked so much of me.
You hold all the power; I need your help, I'll even say please.

Reconciliation can start with such small acts.
It doesn't need to be official to make a big impact.

So going forward, I have a simple request:
I'm asking you to try and do your very best.
I don't expect you to get it right every time.
Making mistakes is okay and just fine.
We're taking on a mountain and it's going to be quite the climb.
So I promise to hold your hand
if you promise to not let go of mine.

Not Perfect

I don't shower every day, I'm not perfect.
I sing off-key when I drive on the highway, I'm not perfect,
I have a dedicated partner but still get crushes every day.
Hey, I'm not perfect.

There are a lot of things I can forgive and understand
as human error,
but not a single one of those comes in the form of
inciting racialized terror.
And I hate to be the bearer of bad news,
but a lack of perfection is a poor excuse
to keep Cornwallis enshrined, regardless of his abuse.
Please, cut him loose.
Do you get what I'm saying, or is my argument obtuse?

How can granting us our humanity be less of a priority
than making the donair the official food of this city?
It's a pity that late-night drunk foods get to be classified as today's
most current issues.
Where are our statues?
May I suggest a few?
Annie Mae Aquash, Donald Marshall Junior, or
Grand Chief Membertou.
See? They all meet the criteria of not being perfect.
They are a group of real apple-tree serpents.
Annie Mae? A divorcée!
Membertou and Marshall? A rebel Catholic and a criminal!
Maybe that last one ended in an acquittal,
but it's because the world thought a L'nu's words were too brittle
to be believed.

It's not news to me.
We have already whitewashed our streets
to rinse off our red-stained hands and feet.
In that park, all paths lead
to his bronzed greed.
I beg and plead.
Can't you see what I see:
that a man decreed
a proclamation on our scalps?
I'm taking you to task,
I'm asking for your help
to heal generations of spiritual welts,
because we were seen as animals
only valued for our pelts.

Today,
we are members of your community.
Show us your humility.
Take my extended branch in unity,
and stop honouring a man who prided himself on his
limitless brutality,
who counted Mi'kmaw fatalities.
Our skins were used as currency.
His legacy built on the belief that our vagrancy
justified replacing our only home, Mi'kma'ki,
with a British colony hell-bent on extinguishing our existence.
But we are persistent!

Centuries later
we are still mounting a resistance,
because no amount of hubris can strip us of our resilience.
We are still here.
I can't make that any more clear.
Don't fear a re-writing of the past but rather how it will look
when this decision is recorded in the history books.

When you turned a blind eye and spied the easy way out.
When you flexed your privileged clout in a bout with a
predetermined outcome.
Because there is no one in that room who looks differently
than you to challenge the status quo, the same old same old.
Is this how Halifax chooses to be bold?

Did you know that the west looked to the east
on how to rid themselves of the Indigenous beast?
They looked to this coast to justify killing kids.
They said that all lice grows from nits.
Even if only a fraction of this is true,
is this the legacy you want immortalized in a statue?
Do you want to be the one to explain this
to my nieces and nephews?

It's time for your minds to be changed,
pride to be checked.
It's time that our voices are given a lot more respect.
I will not fault you for a change of heart on the subject.
Together, we can find a compromise and work it.
Because at the end of the day,
I recognize how hard it is to be perfect.

WHAT AM I Supposed to THINK?

What am I supposed to think
when the hate is spelled out perfectly in internet ink,
calling us "punks" and "drunks"
too lazy to get a job,
collecting handouts so the country can justify ignoring our sobs?

Apparently, it's a well-known fact
that every Indian gets a plaque
inscribed with the words "YOU DON'T HAVE TO PAY TAX."
It might be worth the social axe,
the public attacks,
but it's a myth.
It's time to kick your ignorance.
Please check your facts.

And while our sinister prime minister bathes in the oily black,
he fracks behind our backs,
polluting the waters,
leaving nothing for our sons and daughters.
It's our life's blood flowing through an artery;
once sliced, it can't be cauterized.

But that's not what you've seen
splashed across your TV screens.
So what am I supposed to think,
when the trolls in the polls are so bold as to comment their disdain

but too afraid,
and ashamed,
to leave their real name?

"GET OVER IT!"
is a favourite comment of mine.
As if the mere passing of time
could restore us to our prime,
when we walked with love and balance
instead of being silenced,
and dealt with through violence.

Swapping smudge smoke
for booze and dope,
just trying to cope
with the loss of hope.

We are the products of our histories!
So our dependence should not be a mystery,
because we were taught to be this way.
All of our potential
just taken away.

We have a right to this land.
And so do you,
it's true.
But it's not ours, you see?
Nor is it our majesty's.
To our kids, it belongs.
And their kids.
And their kids' kids,
seven generations strong.

Meet the challenge head on,
so we can experience a new dawn.

A dawn on a day where peace and friendship is the way
we interact,
react,
when we enact our right not to crack the earth open.

Not burn cop cars,
showcase our emotional and cultural scars
from family who spent too much time in bars
trying to find the answers to their fears
in the bottom of their beers.

We are the Wabanaki,
People of the Dawn.
It's a new beginning,
fresh start,
healing heart.
It's just a down-to-the-spirit bruise.
But haven't you seen the news?
We are resilient.
And our love for this land and our people is brilliant,
so bright we shade out the sun.

And so,
those hands,
the ones sent by the Man
who took Annie Mae's for taking a stand.
The ones who took the tools to teach,
the ones with a generational reach,
have arthritis.
And they don't know where the fight is.

So if the air stinks,
it's because the haters are just talking shit.
They've run out of tools in their kit to keep us down.
Just listen to those drums pound.

But that's not the only sound.

Because we have a voice,
and it is our choice to use it.
And use it we will.
So be still,
and listen.

Because it's more than just power.
It's love and knowledge that make the faceless
and the nameless cower.

So let me tell you what I think.
It's time to act out the treaty ink
and link our futures.

Canoe

I don't know how to build a canoe,
whether it be birchbark, plastic, or fibreglass.
It was knowledge that never got passed down to me.

I believed it was a problem with my mentality,
perhaps my mixed blood finding egality.
Because I have been unable to forgive my ignorance,
even though these skills are not a part of my
generational inheritance,
that my fallacy was rooted in my fingertips.
Nails that were chewed down to the quick
were too tired and sore to get a good grip.

They couldn't pull the birch just right.
The bark would tear under their inexperienced might.
Perhaps my eyes would spy trees that were too thin,
filling in the gaps left by those taken too soon by a greedy whim.

Maybe it was my misunderstanding of the seasons
that led me to this cultural treason.
Maybe I picked too early or too late.
The bark keeps splitting, sealing my fate.
I cannot build this canoe,
nobody has shown me what to do.

But there was still the expectation that I should float.
That my blood memory would come with a manual for this boat,
soaked in a culture dispossessed.
And I've been steadily told that what they're giving me
was given to the rest.

"Look! They can sail in all manner of ships."
But they've come from families who remember how to navigate
their skiffs.
They were given schools with direction in their language.
I never had that advantage.

Please.
My jaw is weak from weeping.
The spruce gum is too hard and I'm still teething.
I don't know how to build a canoe!
Tell me what I'm supposed to do.
The water level is rising,
and my life is worth more than simply surviving.

The tools that you've given to me are foreign.
They don't make any sense.
My refusal to use them leaves you incensed and frustrated.
I'm told that you care but I feel placated.
My brothers can't help because they are incarcerated.
And my sisters have all but evaporated.

I don't ask questions about the tools,
I'm told I'm lucky to even be in this school,
so they end up covered in dust.
Those who come after me, just let them rust.

I'm sent to the people who look like me.
Accepting a paycheque so they can eat.
With sore throats from trying to speak.
Office walls let their dreams atrophy.

I don't want their sailboat or his dory.
I don't want a ship full of sails and tales of glory.
Don't tell me it's newer and sleek.
I don't care if you offer me a whole fleet.

I want a canoe that matches my heart.
One that is shaped with my grandfather's bark.
Where the sinew was pulled from my father's skin,
and I weave it through while I remember for him.
I'll use it to paddle through my pain,
pull in bits of my family that I'm trying to save.
But when I speak up, ask for help,
I'm told to behave.

Teach me how to make this canoe.
How to stitch lines that make sense to my spirit.
Don't offer me yachts and rafts,
tell me it's fine because they are all watercraft.
We all need to learn to float,
but don't force me to learn on your boat.

Teach me to build a canoe,
and I'll happily navigate the water with you.

Etuaptmumk

I lost my talk, said Rita Joe.
And me, I was never given the option to know
the feel, the flow of the words as they rolled of my tongue,
giving me the lyrics for how our world was sung.
My perspective was spun using the threads of both
your world and theirs,
left to cobble together a spirit from rags and tears,
painfully aware that I was different.
Through hard work and determination,
I found my Indigenous articulation.
A compilation of two ways make up the sum of me.

You have two eyes,
yet you only have one view.
Your way is best, you would argue.
Centuries of being in the position to subdue those
who would aspire.
They say that the sun never set on the British Empire.
And because we recognized the hubris that defines your story,
we have a sunrise and sunset in our territory.

With my heart and eyes,
I have a completely different view,
The consequence of my skin comes in an entirely different hue.
Don't you see?
Although you represent us,
we think very differently than you.
Because we see the world not through one set of eyes,
but two.

Thousands of years long, we were independent, proud, and strong.
We belonged to this earth,
the way power belongs to money and privilege to birth.
We put our communities first.
But then came the fleets,
filled with those whom you would ironically define today
as "come from away,"
to invade every inch of our world.
To break our spirit and pull the threads that would unfurl us
to catch the way you speak.
But this is not the poem for the retelling of a one-sided history.

Each of our worlds has its strengths.
Yours is in power:
It gets to eat its cake and define race.
It has the ability to unapologetically take up space.
If societal progress is linear,
this society is top tier.
Terra nullius, as though we were never here.
It must be nice to be so confident.
Your strength is that this society is ubiquitous,
built on reified notions of tradition and rhetoric.
Your notions of diversity are ad hoc in nature,
an afterthought feature to an immovable structure.

This isn't a conviction or an acquittal,
just the voice coming from an eye honed to be critical,
who does not shy away from the opportunity to be political.
If you push our two sides of a Venn together, you'll get a circle.

We were never meant to be static.
Like the rivers around us, we shift and change
and remain dynamic.
We bring to the table something that is able to change your world
view and show you what we are capable of.

That a lot can come from a holistic concept of the earth.
You are not a plague nor we a curse or a problem in need
of a solution,
but we've got to rid ourselves of the spiritual dissolution,
the dilution of our treaties written to share this land.
And we ask that you understand that we are the experts
on what we need.
Don't feed us your good intentions.
Carefully laid apologies will not get you an historical exemption.
We plan out our actions for the next seven generations,
and we ask that you do the same.

Open your other set of eyes.
Recognize the pain you have caused.
Take a pause and start breathing.
Welcome to the world of Two-Eyed Seeing.

ENDNOTES

1 As of July 2020, the Washington Redskins, Cleveland Indians, and Edmonton Eskimos have all agreed to change their team names.

2 Sandy Seale was killed by Roy Ebsary. However, Donald Marshall Jr. was sentenced to life in prison for Seale's murder in 1971. Marshall spent eleven years in prison. This wrongful conviction led to a complete overhaul of how evidence is presented to the defence in discovery for criminology laws across Canada.

3 In August 1993, Donald Marshall Jr. was arrested and charged under the Federal Fisheries Act for "illegal" eel fishing in the off-season. He was found guilty on three charges in provincial court. The Supreme Court of Canada reversed the charges in September 1999, in recognition of the hunting and fishing rights promised in the Peace and Friendship Treaties, signed between the Mi'kmaq, Wolastoqiyik, and Peskotomuhkati in 1760–1761. These treaty rights, which apply to Mi'kmaq in Nova Scotia, New Brunswick, PEI, the southern coast of Newfoundland, and Quebec's Gaspé region, are protected today under the Constitution of Canada, section 35.

4 Gabriel Sylliboy was the first elected Grand Chief of the Mi'kmaq Grand Council (1918). In 1927 he was arrested in Unama'ki, otherwise known as Cape Breton Island, Nova Scotia, for off-season hunting and possession of pelts outside of the Whycocomagh reserve where he lived. He argued that the 1752 Peace and Friendship Treaty recognized the right of his people to freely hunt and fish on traditional territories. The judge in this case stayed the conviction, arguing that the Mi'kmaq "were never regarded as an independent power" and for this reason the treaty had no authority. In 2017, the Supreme Court of Canada issued Sylliboy a free pardon posthumously.

5 In the second decision the court elaborated the extension of Aboriginal treaty rights, stating that they are still subject to Canadian law. The second decision, which was claimed to be an "elaboration," was seen as a retreat from the first decision and angered Aboriginal communities. The second decision was issued on a motion for re-hearing the case brought by fishermen's associations in which the court elaborated in particular about such things as the relationship between treaty rights and conservation that had been more implicit in the first decision.

6 R. vs Sparrow, 1990, was the first Supreme Court of Canada case to try section 35 of the Constitution Act (1982). Musqueam commercial fisherman Ronald Edward Sparrow of the Fraser Valley, British Columbia, was charged with using a net longer than his license allowed. After six years of impassioned arguments through every court in the province, in what became known as the Sparrow Decision, Sparrow was cleared of illegal fishing charges by the Supreme Court, which upheld his ancestral right to fishing. The case also led to the creation of criteria, "the Sparrow test," to interpret section 35, providing a method for lawmakers to determine what qualifies as an "Indigenous right."

Author's Note

I often get very nervous when I'm about to perform to an Indigenous audience. I get sweaty and feel nauseated. I am forever waiting for that comment, "You are not good enough to be one of us." I think that is because when I started writing, I did it for the approval of someone else. Perhaps it was my father or the various other Indigenous people who made me feel less than. I took it personally instead of understanding that generations of harm can make people guarded. Furthermore, it's a ludicrous notion to believe everyone will like and agree with me.

My first poems were hard and full of pain. I was denied something that I could never recapture. I had nowhere to put my feelings, so I put them on paper. My poems, for the most part, centred on the greater "Indigenous experience"—as though I was qualified to write it. I took on a political fight and did so with ease. I had the academic training and fancy vocabulary to back up my claims and accusations. However, when it came to writing about my family, friends, obsession, and love, I balked. These poems are intimate, and I feel embarrassed to have people read them. Growing up, personal emotions were frivolous and dismissed as luxuries and annoyances. I can read the awkwardness and uncertainty in these words. I left these poems in because there are generations of Indigenous people who are awkward in and uncertain of how to show love. I hope that sharing these missteps publicly can offer a sense of solidarity to those who are still learning. We are all fucking up and trying again, together. You can be really messed up and still be worthy of love, respect, patience, and kindness.

As I began the work of connecting with my community, my anger shifted. Originally, I was angry at my individual experience. I had (and still have) a strong sense of *This isn't fair*. But I'm learning that this is not just about me. My pain is one drop in the collective bucket of injustice that my community faces every day. I cannot place blame on my Indigenous kin for not loving me hard enough to make all my insecurities disappear. Similarly, I cannot love my community hard enough to heal every hurt they've endured, no matter how much I want to. After all, making it about me meant that I somehow believed my perspective and experiences were more important than those of my community.

I am still angry and hurt. But now these emotions have a purpose and sense of direction. I have softened my edges, though not my wit or words. I am trying very much to live in humility, and I am learning that I'm not very good at it. I have let my hurt and needs spill over and burdened other Indigenous and marginalized people with my pain, and they have held me close and at arm's length. I am grateful for both.

I don't write for other people's approval anymore in the same way, I no longer make myself smaller so others can fit in around me. Love is as infinite as the universe, but it still comes with conditions—just like forgiveness and resilience. This book holds all of the above in a mess of a heart that I am grateful to possess. I found something in these poems. I hope you do too.

Wela'lioq

My father, Redfeather. You gave me my eyes, my adaptability,
   and a legacy.
My sister, Lauren. You gifted me my endurance and my resilience.
My love, Chris. You hold me together when I fall apart.
   You supported me to go on a journey that you could never
   fully understand. Kesalul.
My mom, Pat. You showed me strength and a critical eye.
My community, urban and rez.
My Nation. We are the People of the Dawn. We will always be the first
   light to come out of the darkness.
My Grampy, who never forgot about me.
My friend Killa. You welcomed me into my own community and
   culture with open arms and powwow drives.
My friend Andre. You have held so much of my baggage with kindness
   and patience. I can never repay the perspective and support you
   have given me.
Loni, our long talks over tea made me feel less alone.
Chenise and James, your kindness, care, and laughs connected me to
   more than you intended.
Every Indigenous person who has struggled, made it, found love, lost
   their lives, healed, hurt, grieved, survived, thrived, and endured.
   Your stories have moulded me. You are incredible.
My haters. You have only added fuel to the fire.

ERICA PENTON

REBECCA THOMAS is an award-winning Mi'kmaw poet. She is Halifax's former Poet Laureate (2016–2018) and has been published in multiple journals and magazines. She coordinated the Halifax Slam Poetry team from 2014 to 2017, leading them to three national competitions with the Canadian Festival of Spoken Word. In 2019 she published her first book, *I'm Finding My Talk*, illustrated by Pauline Young, which was named a CBC and *Globe & Mail* Best Book, and shortlisted for two Atlantic Book Awards.